Selected by Frances Clark®

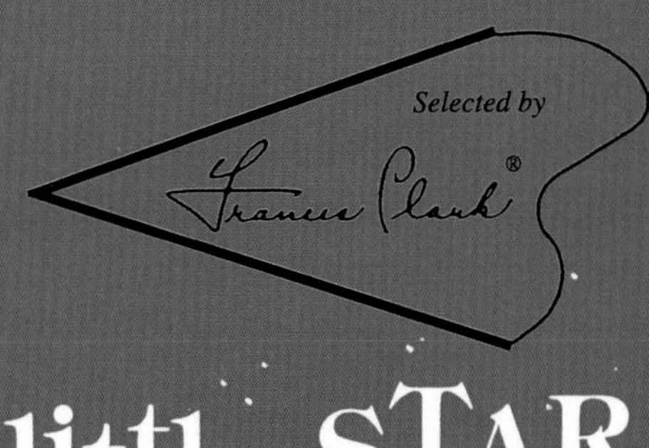

TWINKLE, TWINKLE, little STAR

arranged for three players at one piano

by DAVID KRAEHENBUEHL

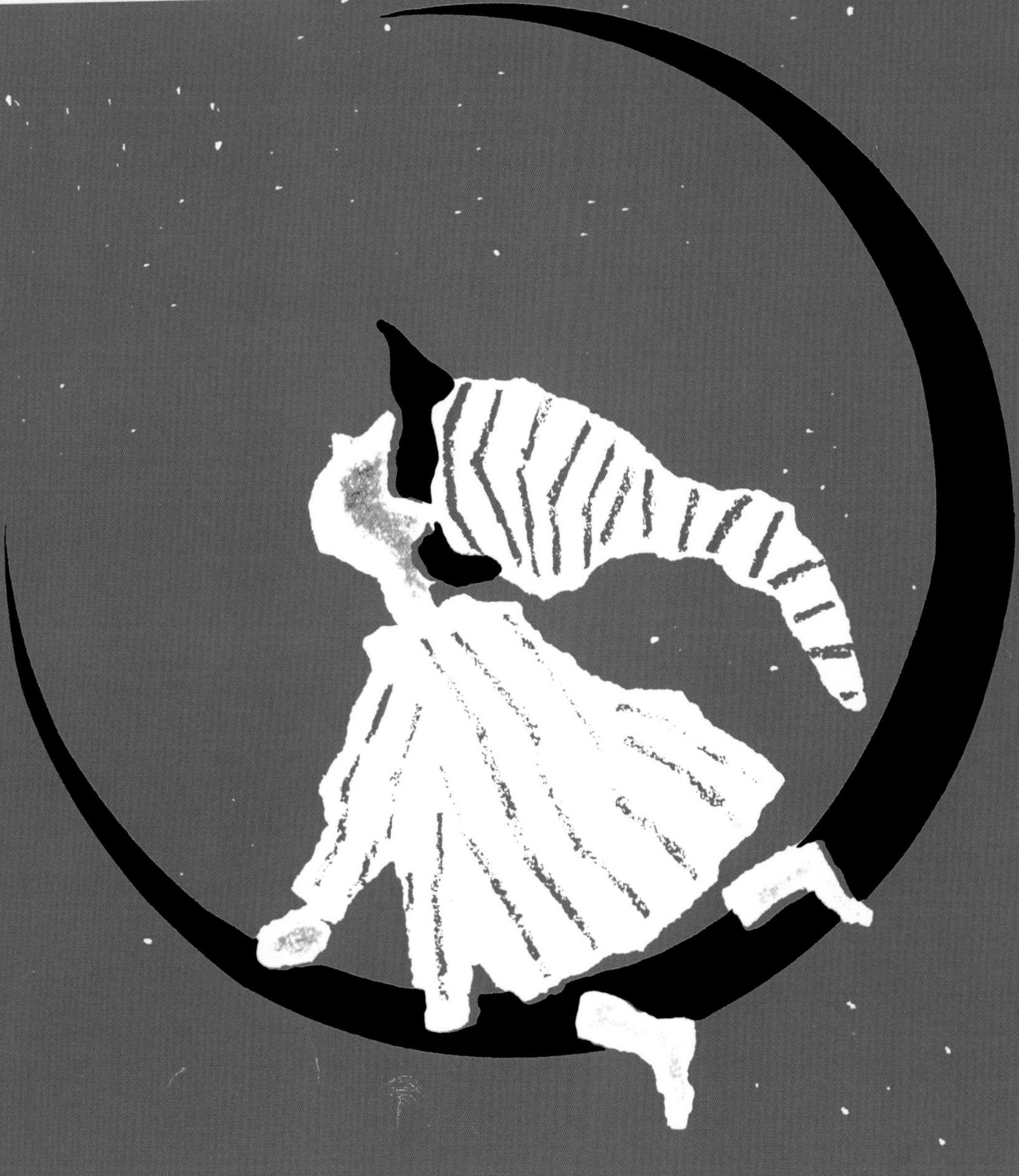

SUMMY-BIRCHARD INC.

Frances Clark® LIBRARY FOR PIANO STUDENTS
SHEET MUSIC

Twinkle, Twinkle, Little Star

Arranged by
David Kraehenbuehl

SUMCO 5571-3
ISBN 0-87487-827-6
3 5 7 9 10 8 6 4

1
2
3
Now, play two octaves higher
Play one octave higher

ISBN-10: 0-87487-827-6
ISBN-13: 978-0-87487-827-1

9 780874 878271

Alfred
alfred.com

SUMMY-BIRCHARD INC.

0827 $3.5

0 29156 18171

ISBN 0-8748-7827-6